Core Math Skills
Measurement and Geometry

Gone Fishing!

Measure Lengths

Celeste Bishop

PowerKiDS press™

NEW YORK

Published in 2014 by The Rosen Publishing Group, Inc.
29 East 21st Street, New York, NY 10010

Book Design: Mickey Harmon

Photo Credits: Cover, p. 5 (boy and man) forestpath/Shutterstock.com; p. 5 (woman) Romain JL/Shutterstock.com;
p. 7 Imaronic/Shutterstock.com; p. 9 Joel Blit/Shutterstock.com; p. 11 (lake) PeJo/Shutterstock.com; p. 11 (bobber)
martellostudio/Shutterstock.com; pp. 13, 15, 21, 22 (fish) Ljesic/Shutterstock.com; pp. 13, 15 (background) cluckva/
Shutterstock.com; pp. 17, 21 (grass) vvita/Shutterstock.com; p. 17 (leaf) PhotoHappiness/Shutterstock.com; p. 17 (long
stick, short stick) vesna cvorovic/Shutterstock.com; p. 19 (snail) pio3/Shutterstock.com; p. 19 (rock) farbled/
Shutterstock.com; p. 19 (grass/dirt) NinaMalyna/Shutterstock.com; pp. 21, 22 (wood) AMINSEN/Shutterstock.com.

Library of Congress Cataloging-in-Publication Data

Bishop, Celeste.
Gone fishing!: measure lengths / by Celeste Bishop.
  p. cm. – (Core math skills: measurement and geometry)
Includes index.
ISBN 978-1-4777-2076-9 (pbk.)
ISBN 978-1-4777-2077-6 (6-pack)
ISBN 978-1-4777-2227-5 (library binding)
1. Measurement–Juvenile literature. 2. Length measurement–Juvenile literature. I. Title.
QC102.B58 2014
516–dc23

Manufactured in the United States of America

CPSIA Compliance Information: Batch #CS13RC: For further information contact Rosen Publishing, New York, New York at 1-800-237-9932.

Word Count: 253

Contents

Away for the Day

Jason, Jen, and their dad go fishing.

Jason is tall.

Jen is taller.

Their dad is the tallest.

They bring their fishing poles.

Jason's pole is long.

Jen's pole is longer.

Their dad's pole is longest.

They're standing from shortest to longest.

Jason   Jen   Dad

On the Boat

There are 3 boats they can use.

One boat is big.

One boat is bigger.

One boat is biggest.

Can you find the biggest one?

They throw their **lines**.

Jason throws his far.

Jen throws hers farther.

Dad throws his farthest.

They're ordered far, farther, and farthest.

Dad

Jen

Jason

They use worms to catch fish.

Their dad's fish is 5 worms long.

Jen's fish is 6 worms long.

Jason's fish is 8 worms long.

They're ordered long, longer, and longest.

13

They catch even more fish!

This time their dad's fish is 7 worms long.

Jen's fish is 3 worms long.

Jason's fish is 4 worms long.

Who catches the longest fish?

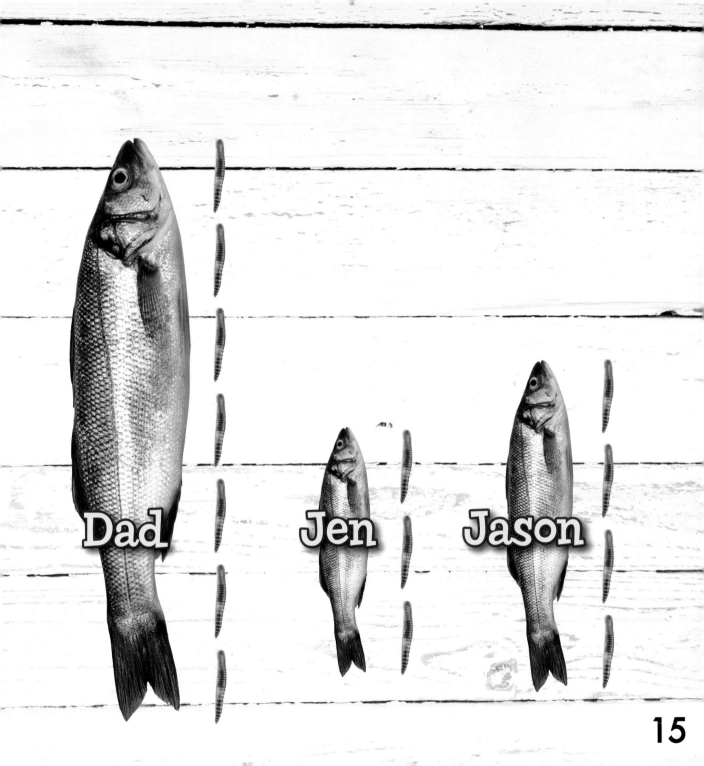

Dad

Jen

Jason

15

Back on Shore

Jason finds a leaf.

Then, Jen finds two **sticks**.

The first stick is 4 leaves long.

The second stick is 6 leaves long.

The second stick is longer.

Later, Jason finds a snail.

Jen finds rocks.

The first rock is 5 snails long.

The second rock is 2 snails long.

The first rock is longer.

They find 2 **picnic** tables for lunch.

One table is 5 fish long.

The second table is 3 fish long.

Which table is longer?

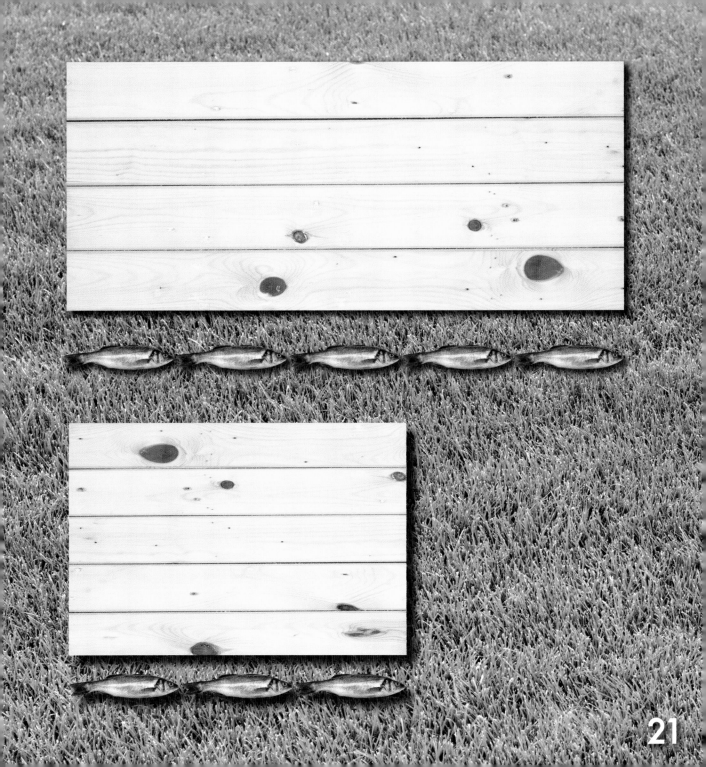

Jason and Jen had a great day with their dad!

They bring 3 fish home for their mom.

Which one is the longest?

Glossary

line (LYN) The string on a fishing pole.

picnic (PIHK-nihk) A meal eaten outside for fun.

stick (STIHK) A thin piece of wood from a tree.

Index

Due to the changing nature of Internet links, The Rosen Publishing Group, Inc., has developed an online list of websites related to the subject of this book. This site is updated regularly. Please use this link to access the list: **www.powerkidslinks.com/cms/mg/gfi**